TWO CULTURES?
THE SIGNIFICANCE OF C. P. SNOW

WITH AN ESSAY ON
SIR CHARLES SNOW'S REDE LECTURE

TWO CULTURES?
THE SIGNIFICANCE
OF C. P. SNOW

BY

F. *Frank* R. LEAVIS

FELLOW OF DOWNING COLLEGE, CAMBRIDGE

Being the Richmond Lecture, 1962
With a New Preface for the American Reader

And an Essay on
SIR CHARLES SNOW'S REDE LECTURE

BY

MICHAEL YUDKIN

PANTHEON BOOKS
A Division of Random House
NEW YORK

FIRST PRINTING

DESIGN BY HERBERT H. JOHNSON

CONTENTS

BIOGRAPHICAL NOTE

Dr. F. R. Leavis was born in Cambridge, England, in 1895, and since that time has lived and worked entirely in and for Cambridge. There, at the Perse School, under the famous headmaster Dr. W. H. D. Rouse, whose distinction it was to have insisted that Greek and Latin be taught and learned as living languages, he took the normal courses in classics, English literature, French and German. He was awarded a history scholarship to Emmanuel College, Cambridge, where he studied history and English. He took his B.A. degree in 1921, and his Ph.D. in English literature three years later.

Traditionally, Cambridge (with Oxford) occupies in England a position for which there is no American equivalent. It has its pick of all the most intelligent students in the country, and is enormously influential in every aspect of English cultural life. The English 'Honours' course (the so-called English Tripos) had been instituted towards the end of the First World War, and offered a study of literature ('literature, life and thought' is one of the rubrics), rather than the traditional 'language and literature' where the emphasis lay so heavily on medieval Latin, Anglo-Saxon, and Middle English.

This offered possibilities for the teaching and studying of English literature and civilization—and for influencing the movement of civilization from a center which Dr. Leavis, like Matthew Arnold before him, felt the need of—available nowhere else in England. Dr. Leavis remained in Cambridge, and except for three years (1927-30) when he held a probationary lectureship in the English faculty, he supported himself and his family up to 1936 entirely on the uncertainties of free-lance teaching. In 1929 he married Q. D. Roth, a research student whose work was later published as *Fiction and the Reading Public*. Dr. Leavis's own early publications included two pamphlets, *D. H. Lawrence* (1930) and *Mass Civilization and Minority Culture* (1930), both collected in *For Continuity* (1933); and *New Bearings in English Poetry* (1932). These books were important both in themselves and in being so closely related to the collaborative discussion and effort which lies behind the quarterly review *Scrutiny*.

In 1932 a group comprised largely of research students and centering at the Leavises' house, founded *Scrutiny* 'on the assumption that a magazine in which intelligent men and women can exchange and refine their ideas, and which provides a focus of intellectual interests, will perform a service attempted by no other paper.' This effort to maintain in Cambridge a community of critical intelligence which would make it possible for people widely separated in space and interests to discover 'the best that is known and thought in the world' has been Dr. Leavis's main work. His books —*Revaluation* (1936), *The Great Tradition* (1948), *The Common Pursuit* (1952), and *D. H. Lawrence, Novelist* (1956)—grew out of his work for *Scrutiny* and his teaching. He has also written specifically on education: *Culture and Environment* (1933), a handbook for schoolteachers written with Denys Thompson, and *Education and the University* (1943), an outline for a proposed course in English literature. It is possible to assert that Dr. Leavis has had as profound and salutary an influence on humane education in England as any single person since Erasmus. Dr. Leavis continued to edit *Scrutiny* until 1953, when it ceased publication. At present it is being reprinted in its entirety by the Cambridge University Press, with a Retrospect by Dr. Leavis. It is among the most important literary facts of this century.

In 1936 Dr. Leavis was elected into a fellowship at Downing College, and appointed to an Assistant University Lectureship in English. Since that time, and without sabbatical leave, he has lectured in the English faculty and taught for Downing, creating in that college the most influential center of literary studies in England. In 1947 he was appointed to a full University Lectureship in English, and in 1959, in recognition of his achievements, to a University Readership in English. In 1961 Dr. Leavis was nominated for the Chair of Poetry at Oxford, but lost the election to Robert Graves. In 1962 Dr. Leavis reached the retiring age, and was elected an honorary fellow of Downing. He continues to teach for Downing and a number of other colleges in the university.

PREFATORY NOTE

THE ABUNDANT adverse comment directed against my lecture hasn't advanced the argument by leaving me something to answer. *The Spectator* was indulgent when it called the mass of correspondence it printed a 'debate.' I say 'adverse comment' because to say 'criticism' would be inappropriate: the case I presented wasn't dealt with —there was no attempt to deal with it. The angry, abusive and strikingly confident utterances of Snow's supporters merely illustrated the nature of the world or 'culture' that had made Snow a mind, a sage, and a major novelist. 'Without thinking they respond alike.' The confidence is remarkable and significant because the demonstrators see themselves, unmistakably, as an intellectual *élite* and pre-eminently capable of grounded conviction, and yet, when they sense criticism by which their distinction and standing are implicitly denied, can only, with the flank-rubber's response, enact an involuntary corroboration of the criticism.

The lecture and its reception go on being referred to a great deal: there is reason, I think, for making generally accessible in print what I actually said. The issues are alive and momentous, and Sir Charles Snow's *The Two*

Cultures seems likely to go on circulating—in schools and elsewhere. I have to thank Mr. Yudkin for letting me print his article along with my lecture. It didn't come to my notice till the lecture had been delivered and had appeared in *The Spectator*. And Mr. Yudkin's criticism was wholly independent of mine: it had been published (in the *Cambridge Review*) a good while before my Richmond Lecture had been thought of.

It might in a sense have been said to make my lecture unnecessary. But it puts what seems to me the unanswerable case against Snow from another approach than mine: Mr. Yudkin is a research scientist (biochemist). And such a concurrence (for it is essentially that) arrived at from approaches so different seems to me to give decided point to the printing of the two critical formulations together. In my lecture, of course, my criticism of *The Two Cultures* subserves a preoccupation with a positive theme and advocacy of my own. But my argument *is,* very largely, the criticism, which is inseparable from the presentment of the positive theme. I know too, from many letters I have received from both sides of the Atlantic, that Snow, though widely thought of as 'public relations' man for Science, is far from being regarded with favour by all scientists. Nor had I supposed, or meant to imply, otherwise. In any case, I feel it impossible to believe that scientists in considerable numbers will not acclaim Mr. Yudkin's criticism of Snow as sound—and salutary.

I have said enough by way of explaining the decision to print the two independently conceived critiques in association.

My LECTURE was given in England. The above para-
graphs, written as a 'Prefatory Note,' were addressed to
a British public. I knew, however, that Snow had received much publicity in America, and that Professor
Lionel Trilling, in the New York review *Commentary*
(June 1962), had thought it worth while criticising my
lecture for a public that, for the most part, couldn't have
read it. And when, in the above 'Note,' I made my
dismissing comment on my critics I wasn't intending to
except Trilling: it seemed to me that he too had made
no attempt to deal as a disinterested critic with what I
had actually said. That is, no rejoinder was called for;
he had my answer there already before him in my lecture. A general charge he brings against me is the one
thing I think worth adverting to in particular here. I will
say a little about it because I can at the same time in-
dicate all there is any point in saying about another
critic of my lecture whom I know to have addressed an
American audience: Mr. Richard Wollheim in *Partisan
Review* (Spring 1962).

'There can be no two opinions,' says Professor Trilling, 'about the tone in which Dr. Leavis deals with Sir
Charles.' More particularly the charge is that my references to Snow's novels were gratuitous, not being
necessary to my theme and argument. They are cruel in
their gratuitousness, we are to gather: they are expressed, characteristically (Mr. Trilling intimates), in a
way calculated to cause unnecessary pain and offence. I
have to comment that, in thus lending himself to the gen-

eral cry that I have 'attacked' Snow (and 'attack' goes
with the suggestion that I have indulged in an unpleasant
display of personal animus), Mr. Trilling, who passes
as a vindicator of the critical function, seems to me
guilty of *la trahison des clercs*. His attitude would make
the essential work of the critic today impossible. It
belongs to the ethos I was intent on challenging.

In my lecture I deal with certain menacing characteris-
tics of our civilisation. Snow, I start by emphasising, is
a *portent;* a portent in that, while he is in himself without distinction of any kind, so that it is ridiculous to
credit him with any capacity for serious thinking about
the problems on which he offers to advise the world, he
has been accepted very widely in England (and in
America too, I believe) as a powerful and diversely
gifted mind and an authoritative voice of wisdom. If
one calls attention to the clear truth about such a
portent in a way that exposes to the full light of publicity the unanswerableness of the constatation, then,
of course, the critical or hygienic process that achieved
the result aimed at may fairly be called (what it necessarily had to be) drastic, and the portent as person may
very well feel 'wounded,' leaving his friends to accuse
one of 'cruelty.' But those critics who call me, the per-
petrator of the Richmond Lecture, cruel—what excuse
have they? None, I think. But the significance is clear:
they have played their part in the creating of the portent,
they have underwritten—at least tacitly—the Intellect
and the Sage, and they cry out with so intense an animus
against the damaging constatation because its truth is so
unanswerably clear. The unanswerableness is the 'cruelty' and is what has 'wounded' Snow. It would have
been less 'cruel' if it had been accompanied, as it was

not, by the animus that impels the intention to hurt.[1]

My lecture has no personal animus in it: the kind of drastic finality I aimed at in my dismissal of the Intellect and Sage was incompatible with that. But, of course, if by a sharpness, clarity and cogency of challenge that make it hardly possible not to see the 'cruel' truth you undo the publicity-work that has made a great public figure out of a person of undistinguished capacities, that person must inevitably feel that he has suffered an odious experience—one that he will identify with an unfeeling and destructive 'attack.' For anyone, however, who has made a name as concerned for a high intellectual standard and critical integrity to join with the 'victim's' friends and allies in passing on the public that kind of identification as a just criticism of the critic is (as I have said) no better than *trahison des clercs*.

For the supersession, in what should be the field of real intellectual and spiritual authority, of serious criteria by the power of creating publicity-values is a frightening manifestation of the way our civilisation is going. It is a concomitant of the technological revolution. The kind of standards that concern the literary critic (say) can be 'there' for him to appeal to only in the existence of a public that can respond intelligently to the challenge and make its response felt. I have no doubt that there are in England today (I confine myself to speaking of my own country) the elements of such a public; there are a great many cultivated and responsible individuals, and they may be regarded as forming some sort of intellectual community. But it is not in anything

[1] I was not warned of the editor's intention to insert cartoons into the text of my lecture as printed in *The Spectator,* and he had my indignant protest.

like a full sense a community; the consequences of the technological revolution preclude its being a public in the way the critic needs.

Organs addressing the 'educated' public require in our time large circulations in order to satisfy the advertisement manager and subsist. The so-called 'quality' Sunday papers (*The Observer* and *The Sunday Times*), for instance, must attract and hold their million readers, and they can hope to do so only by catering at a level of appeal realistically calculated in relation to a mass public of the kind (that of the class-consciously superior middle classes, business and professional). They make a show, that is, of observing the standards of taste, education and serious intellectual interest of *haute culture,* while actually supplying 'magazine' diversion and gossip-fodder for the relaxed middle-brow. They maintain in their review pages—an aspect of this cultural phenomenon that, with my eye on my theme, I have to emphasise—the air and the reputation of performing the critical function at the highest level, their reviewers being (it is to be understood) of the intellectual *élite.* And indeed they are, if anything properly to be called an intellectual *élite* anywhere presents itself in British journalism. The critical function is performed at no higher level in the intellectual weeklies, where in fact we find not only the same kind of writer, but very largely the same names.

And here I come to an observation that must be seen, I suppose, as pointing to a marked difference between what an American with my interests and anxieties would report and what one has to reckon with in the aspect of British civilisation I myself am contemplating. For America is not a tight little island, and Great Britain is.

How little and how tight is brought home to one when, thinking that the preposterous and menacing absurdity of a C. P. Snow's consecrated public standing shouldn't remain longer undealt with, one challenges recognition for the patent fact that the Emperor is naked. One finds arrayed against one a comprehensive system of personal relations, the members of which (even though the use of the Christian name may not mean much[2]) know they 'belong,' and observe a corresponding code.

The system has its literary-journalistic organs and foci and its institutional centres, and at the midmost, wholly in its possession on the literary side, is the B.B.C., with its organ *The Listener*. The B.B.C. is an immensely potent means of giving general currency to the values of the metropolitan literary world—that which Snow calls 'the traditional culture,' meaning the *élite* he supposes himself to mingle with in the *New Statesman* circle— and of getting them accepted as the 'best that is thought and known in our time.' These values can be the merest publicity-creations, created by iteration, symphonic suggestion, and the authority of the 'intellectuals' of the system, as Snow the Sage and distinguished novelist was.

Not that I suppose there weren't a number of his literary-intellectual friends who preferred not to seek opportunities to express publicly a conviction of his creative genius. For his incapacity as a novelist plainly is what, in my lecture, I say it is—total. He seems to me almost unreadable. Yet a great number of copies of his novels is to be found in every public library, and they go out a great deal. The explanation can be seen in the

---

[2] It is a significant index. Thus Dame Edith Sitwell pronounced for publication, 'Dr. Leavis only attacked Charles because he is famous and writes good English.'

fact that Snow has been made a major subject for lecture-directed study in W.E.A. classes[3] and in adult education generally. And it is not only Snow's Rede Lecture that is pushed for devout study on the young (our future educated class) in the upper forms of grammar schools; his novels are too. Are they not contemporary classics? And does not the British Council endorse that estimate?—the British Council, that characteristic British institution which, financed out of public funds and well-regarded by the Foreign Office, fosters the repute of British culture abroad (though not, I believe, in the United States), and, for the instruction of the world, issues on British writers (picked by itself) brochures that sell immensely at home and are to be found in every Cambridge bookshop.

A scrutiny of this British Council literature of guidance and currency-promotion will reveal that the ethos, the sense of values, the critical enlightenment it serves are those of what I have called the metropolitan literary world—the cultural world of Sir Charles Snow's 'literary intellectual.' The British Council, in fact, is another institutional centre for that world, and, like the B.B.C., is taken full advantage of as such. How much that is other than robust good conscience there may be in all this it is, in the nature of things, such a state of affairs having become established, difficult to say; in fact, the question hardly applies. But the system is quick to react to the threat represented by any criticism that seems to challenge its ethos; by any implicit reminder, that is, of serious standards. Such reminders cannot be tolerated; it is a matter of self-preservation. The resources of the system are deployed against the offending critic or 'in-

[3] Workers' Educational Association, a democratic organization for adult education.

fluence'; if he can't be suppressed he must be, by any means, discredited.

For the 'literary world' has to maintain its sense, and the general illusion, of its own comprehensiveness. It is immune from control by the educated public—the intellectual and spiritual community in which, so far as in this technological civilisation it can be effectively appealed to and can make its response felt, standards are 'there' to be evoked by the critic. The 'literary world' is its own public—the only one it, normally, is conscious of. It hates the suggestion that there might be another, one to be feared: a real educated public that doesn't take the 'literary world' seriously.

The 'literary world,' in fact, with its command of all the means of publicity, virtually shuts off the educated public from effective existence. This public, in any serious sense of the noun, is only a potential public. It has no part in the formation of contemporary taste, no power to influence or to check—I am thinking of what passes for educated taste.

Though I spoke of the 'literary world' as 'metropolitan,' I wasn't forgetting that, most significantly, an essential element in it (and I don't mean my 'literary' to be taken in a narrow sense—I am thinking of what, borrowing a licence from Snow, I will call the whole publicity-created culture) belongs to the universities. I refer to this fact and its significance in the close of my lecture. That Snow should have been chosen as Rede Lecturer at Cambridge, that his lecture should have passed there as a distinguished intellectual performance, and that his novels should be supposed by Classical dons to be contemporary literature—these things can't be seen as surprising: they are representative. It wouldn't be at all ridiculous to conjecture that Snow might have decisive

influence in academic appointments—and on the side of
the humanities.

Here, then, we have the cultural consequences of the
technological revolution. And to Mr. Richard Wollheim,
who charges me (so far as I can understand him) with
insidious and significant evasion in not saying clearly
whether I am for a high material standard of living or
against it, I reply that the problem I am concerned with
cannot be reduced to those terms, and that in insisting
that it can he ignores the whole theme, argument and
substance of my lecture, and that, if he really reads it,
he will find my answer to the given charge in the place
where I deal with Snow's use of 'Neo-Luddite'—and
elsewhere. What I have contended, giving my reasons as
forcibly as in an hour's discourse I could, is that we
mustn't regard these cultural consequences as inevitable,
or acquiesce in their being accepted mechanically and
unconsciously, and that a preoccupation and an effort
of a very different kind from any contemplated by Snow
are necessary. And I have to add that, in his ability to
ignore my theme as he does, Mr. Wollheim, who is a
sociologist, seems to me himself a portent.

As for Mr. Trilling's charge that my bringing Snow's
novels into my argument was a gratuitously offensive ir-
relevance, I find it hard to understand how he can have
persuaded himself that he was justified in making it. Is
it true that, as I have heard, he has committed himself
in print to a favourable opinion of Snow the novelist? If
so, does he still hold it?

And Mr. Wollheim's suggestion ('the sheltered atmos-
phere of the hall at Downing College') that the Press
and the B.B.C. were excluded from my lecture because
I wished to be protected against critical reactions is
oddly wide of the mark. The Richmond Lecture is

private, and I, who was merely the person invited to give it this year, certainly didn't want it to be made the occasion of the ugly kind of publicity it actually got—and would inevitably get, if the Press were given a chance. And I was intent on ensuring that my actual theme and argument should be really attended to. I should have indeed been a fool if I had thought that giving the journalists an opportunity was likely to further that aim. My purpose was to see to the publication of the full text myself. It will be supposed that, in so far as I had been sanguine, Mr. Trilling's and Mr. Wollheim's responses to the text as it appeared in *The Spectator* brought me some disillusion.

F. R. LEAVIS

TWO CULTURES?
THE SIGNIFICANCE OF C. P. SNOW

WITH AN ESSAY ON
SIR CHARLES SNOW'S REDE LECTURE

TWO CULTURES?

The Significance of C. P. Snow

I F CONFIDENCE in oneself as a master-mind, qualified by capacity, insight and knowledge to pronounce authoritatively on the frightening problems of our civilisation, is genius, then there can be no doubt about Sir Charles Snow's. He has no hesitations. Of course, anyone who offers to speak with inwardness and authority on both science and literature will be conscious of more than ordinary powers, but one can imagine such consciousness going with a certain modesty—with a strong sense, indeed, of a limited range and a limited warrant. The peculiar quality of Snow's assurance expresses itself in a pervasive tone; a tone of which one can say that, while only genius could justify it, one cannot readily think of genius adopting it. It is the tone we have (in so far as it can be given in an isolated sentence) here:

> The only writer of world-class who seems to have had an understanding of the industrial revolution was Ibsen in his old age: and there wasn't much that old man didn't understand.

Clearly, there is still less Sir Charles Snow doesn't understand: he pays the tribute with authority. We take

the implication and take it the more surely at its full
value because it carries the *élan,* the essential inspiration,
of the whole self-assured performance. Yet Snow is in
fact portentously ignorant. No doubt he could himself
pass with ease the tests he proposes for his literary
friends with the intimation that *they* would fail them, and
so expose themselves as deplorably less well educated in
respect of science than he, though a scientist, can claim
to be in respect of literature. I have no doubt that *he*
can define a machine-tool and state the second law of
thermodynamics. It is even possible, I suppose (though
I am obliged to say that the evidence seems to me to be
against it), that he could make a plausible show of being
inward with the Contradiction of Parity, that esoteric
upshot of highly subtle experiment which, he suggests, if
things were well with our education, would have been a
major topic at our High Tables. But of history, of the
nature of civilisation and the history of its recent developments, of the human history of the Industrial
Revolution, of the human significances entailed in that
revolution, of literature, of the nature of that kind of
collaborative human creativity of which literature is the
type, it is hardly an exaggeration to say that Snow exposes complacently a complete ignorance.

The judgment I have to come out with is that not only
is he not a genius; he is intellectually as undistinguished
as it is possible to be. If that were all, and Snow were
merely negligible, there would be no need to say so in
any insistent public way, and one wouldn't choose to do
it. But I used the adverb 'portentously' just now with
full intention: Snow is a portent. He is a portent in that,
being in himself negligible, he has become for a vast
public on both sides of the Atlantic a master-mind and a
sage. His significance is that he has been accepted—or

perhaps the point is better made by saying 'created': he has been created as authoritative intellect by the cultural conditions manifested in his acceptance. Really distinguished minds are themselves, of course, *of* their age; they are responsive at the deepest level to its peculiar strains and challenges: that is why they are able to be truly illuminating and prophetic and to influence the world positively and creatively. Snow's relation to the age is of a different kind; it is characterised not by insight and spiritual energy, but by blindness, unconsciousness and automatism. He doesn't know what he means, and doesn't know he doesn't know. That is what his intoxicating sense of a message and a public function, his inspiration, amounts to. It is not any challenge he thinks of himself as uttering, but the challenge he *is,* that demands our attention. The commentary I have to make on him is necessarily drastic and dismissive; but don't, I beg, suppose that I am enjoying a slaughterous field-day. Snow, I repeat, is in himself negligible. My preoccupation is positive in spirit. Snow points to its nature when he turns his wisdom upon education and the university.

I have not been quick to propose for myself the duty of dealing with him: that will, I hope, be granted. *The Two Cultures and the Scientific Revolution,* the Rede Lecture which established him as an Intellect and a Sage, was given at this ancient university in 1959. I turned over the pages of the printed lecture in the show-room of the Cambridge University Press, was struck by the mode of expression Snow found proper and natural, perceived plainly enough what kind of performance the lecture was, and had no inclination to lay down three and sixpence. To my surprise, however, it rapidly took on the standing of a classic. It was continually being referred

to—and not only in the Sunday papers—as if Snow, that
rarely qualified and profoundly original mind, had given
trenchant formulation to a key contemporary truth.
What brought me to see that I must overcome the inner
protest, and pay my three and sixpence, was the realis-
ing, from marking scholarship scripts, that sixth-form
masters were making their bright boys read Snow as
doctrinal, definitive and formative—and a good examination investment.

Well, I bought the lecture last summer, and, having
noted that it had reached the sixth printing, read it
through. I was then for the first time in a position to
know how mild a statement it is to say that *The Two
Cultures* exhibits an utter lack of intellectual distinction
and an embarrassing vulgarity of style. The lecture, in
fact, with its show of giving us the easily controlled spon-
taneity of the great man's talk, exemplifies kinds of bad
writing in such richness and so significant a way that
there would, I grant, be some point in the schoolmaster's
using it as a text for elementary criticism; criticism of
the style, here, becomes, as it follows down into analysis,
criticism of the thought, the essence, the pretensions.

The intellectual nullity is what constitutes any diffi-
culty there may be in dealing with Snow's panoptic
pseudo-cogencies, his parade of a thesis: a mind to be
argued with—that is not there; what we have is something other. Take that crucial term 'culture,' without
which and the work he relies on it to do for him Snow
would be deprived of his seer's profundity and his show
of a message. His use of it focuses for us (if I may be
permitted what seems to me an apt paradox) the intellectual nullity; it confronts us unmistakably with the
absence of the thought that is capable of posing problems
(let alone answering them). The general nature of his

position and his claim to authority are well known: there
are the two uncommunicating and mutually indifferent
cultures, there is the need to bring them together, and
there is C. P. Snow, whose place in history is that he
has them both, so that we have in him the paradigm of
the desired and necessary union.

Snow is, of course, a—no, I can't say that; he isn't:
Snow thinks of himself as a novelist. I don't want to dis-
cuss that aspect of him, but I can't avoid saying something. The widespread belief that he is a distinguished
novelist (and that it should be widespread is significant
of the conditions that produced him) has certainly its
part in the success with which he has got himself accepted as a mind. The seriousness with which he takes
himself as a novelist is complete—if seriousness can be
so ineffably blank, so unaware. Explaining why he
should have cut short a brilliant career (we are to understand) as a scientist, he tells us that it had always been
his vocation to be a writer. And he assumes with a happy
and undoubting matter-of-factness—the signs are un-
mistakable—that his sense of vocation has been trium-
phantly vindicated and that he is beyond question a
novelist of a high order (of 'world-class' even, to adopt
his own idiom). Confidence so astonishingly enjoyed
might politely be called memorable—if one could imagine the memory of Snow the novelist long persisting;
but it won't, it can't, in spite of the British Council's
brochure on him (he is a British Council classic). I say
'astonishingly enjoyed,' for as a novelist he doesn't exist;
he doesn't begin to exist. He can't be said to know what
a novel is. The nonentity is apparent on every page of his
fictions—consistently manifested, whatever aspect of a
novel one looks for. I am trying to remember where I
heard (can I have dreamed it?) that they are composed

for him by an electronic brain called Charlie, into which
the instructions are fed in the form of the chapter-head-
ings. However that may be, he—or the brain (if that's
the explanation)—can't do any of the things the power
to do which makes a novelist. He tells you what you are
to take him as doing, but he can give you no more than
the telling. When the characters are supposed to fall in
love you are told they do, but he can't show it happening.
Abundant dialogue assures you that this is the novelistic
art, but never was dialogue more inept; to imagine it
spoken is impossible. And Snow is helpless to suggest
character in speech. He announces in his chapter-head-
ings the themes and developments in which we are to
see the significance of what follows, but what follows
adds nothing to the effect of the announcement, and
there is no more significance in the completed book than
there is drama—or life. It is not merely that Snow can't
make his characters live for us—that he lacks *that*
creative power; the characters as he thinks of them are
so impoverished in the interests they are supposed to
have and to represent that even if they had been made
to live, one would have asked of them, individually and
in the lump: 'What of life is there here, and what significance capable of engaging an educated mind *could* be
conveyed through such representatives of humanity?'

Among the most current novels of Snow's are those
which offer to depict from the inside the senior academic
world of Cambridge, and they suggest as characteristic
of that world lives and dominant interests of such un-
relieved and cultureless banality that, if one could credit
Snow's art with any power of imaginative impact, one
would say that he had done his university much harm—
for this is a time when the image of the ancient university
that is entertained at large matters immensely. Even

when he makes a suspect piece of research central to his plot, as in that feeble exercise, *The Affair,* he does no more than a very incompetent manufacturer of whodunnits could do: no corresponding intellectual interest comes into the novel; science is a mere word, the vocation merely postulated. It didn't take a brilliant research scientist to deal with the alleged piece of research as Snow deals with it—or a scientist of any kind. Both George Eliot and Lawrence could have made such a theme incomparably more real.

What the novelist really believes in, the experience he identifies his profoundest ego with bcause it makes him feel himself a distinguished man and a lord of life, is given us in Lewis Eliot. Eliot has inhabited the Corridors of Power; that is what really matters; that is what qualifies him to look down upon these dons, the scientists as well as the literary intellectuals, with a genially 'placing' wisdom from above; there we have the actual Snow, who, I repeat, is a portent of our civilisation; there we have the explanation of his confident sense of importance, which, in an extraordinary way, becomes where his writing is concerned a conviction of genius: he has known from inside the Corridors of Power. That he has really *been* a scientist, that science as such has ever, in any important inward way, existed for him, there is no evidence in his fiction.

And I have to say now that in *The Two Cultures and the Scientific Revolution* there is no evidence, either. The only presence science has is as a matter of external reference, entailed in a show of knowledgeableness. Of qualities that one might set to the credit of a scientific training there are none. As far as the internal evidence goes, the lecture was conceived and written by someone who had not had the advantage of an intellectual discipline of any kind. I was on the point of illustrating this truth from Snow's way with the term 'culture'—a term so important for his purposes. By way of enforcing his testimony that the scientists 'have their own culture,' he tells us: 'This culture contains a great deal of argument, usually much more rigorous, and almost always at a higher conceptual level, than literary persons' arguments.' But the argument of Snow's Rede Lecture is at an immensely *lower* conceptual level, and incomparably more loose and inconsequent, than any I myself, a literary person, should permit in a group discussion I was conducting, let alone a pupil's essay.

Thought, it is true, in the field in which Snow challenges us, doesn't admit of control by strict definition of the key terms; but the more fully one realises this the more aware will one be of the need to cultivate a vigilant responsibility in using them, and an alert consciousness of any changes of force they may incur as the argument passes from context to context. And what I have to say is that Snow's argument proceeds with so extreme a *naïveté* of unconsciousness and irresponsibility that to call it a movement of thought is to flatter it.

Take the confident ease of his way with what he calls 'the Literary Culture,' that one of his opposed pair which, as a novelist, he feels himself qualified to present to us with a peculiar personal authority. He identifies 'the Literary Culture' with, to use his own phrase, the 'literary intellectual'—by which he means the modish literary world; his 'intellectual' is the intellectual of the *New Statesman* circle and the reviewing in the Sunday papers. Snow accepts this 'culture' implicitly as the *haute culture* of our time; he takes it as representing the age's finer consciousness so far as a culture ignorant of science can. He, we are to understand, has it, and at the same time the scientific culture; he unites the two. I can't help remarking that this suggested equivalence (equivalence at any rate in reality) must constitute for me, a literary person, the gravest suspicion regarding the scientific one of Snow's two cultures. For his 'literary culture' is something that those genuinely interested in literature can only regard with contempt and resolute hostility. Snow's 'literary intellectual' is the enemy of art and life.

Note with what sublime, comic and frightening ease (for this sage is after all a Cambridge man) Snow, without any sense of there having been a shift, slips from his 'literary culture' into 'the traditional culture.' The feat of innocent unawareness is striking and significant enough when he is talking of the contemporary scene. But when, with the same ease, he carries the matter-of-fact identification into the past—'the traditional culture,' he tells us, with reference to the Industrial Revolution, 'didn't notice: or when it did notice, didn't like what it saw'— the significance becomes so portentous as to be hardly credible. But Snow, we must remind ourselves, *is* frightening in his capacity of representative phenomenon. He knows nothing of history. He pronounces about it with as complete a confidence as he pronounces about literature (French, Russian and American as well as English), but he is equally ignorant of both. He has no notion of the changes in civilisation that have produced his 'literary culture' and made it possible for C. P. Snow to enjoy a status of distinguished intellectual, have the encouragement of knowing that his Rede Lecture is earnestly studied in sixth forms, and be (with practical consequences) an authority in the field of higher education: things that the real, the living 'traditional culture' (for there is a reality answering to that phrase) can no more countenance today that it could have foreseen them in the nineteenth century.

The intellectual nullity apparent in his way with the term 'culture' is only emphasized for us when, coming to his other culture, that of the scientist, he makes, as himself a scientist, his odd show of a concern for a 'high conceptual level.' 'At one pole,' he says, 'the scientific culture really is a culture, not only in an intellectual, but also in an anthropological sense.' The offered justification for that 'anthropological sense' is given, we find, if we examine the context, in this sentence: 'Without thinking about it they respond alike.' Snow adds: 'That is what a culture means.' We needn't bother one way or the other about the 'anthropological'; what is certain is that Snow gives us here a hint worth taking up. He, of course, is supposed to be thinking, and thinking profoundly, in that Rede Lecture, but actually it is a perfect document of the kind of 'culture,' to use his word, that he here defines—defines, even though unconscious of the full significance of what he says, the formal definition getting its completion and charge from the whole context —that is, from the actual performance. His unconsciousness is an essential characteristic. 'Without thinking, they respond alike': Snow's habits as an intellectual and a sage were formed in such a milieu. Thinking is a difficult art and requires training and practice in any given field. It is a pathetic and comic—and menacing— illusion on Snow's part that he is capable of thought on the problems he offers to advise us on. If his lecture has any value for use in schools—or universities—it is as a document for the study of cliché.

We think of cliché commonly as a matter of style. But style is a habit of expression, and a habit of expression that runs to the cliché tells us something adverse about the quality of the thought expressed. 'History is merciless to failure': Snow makes play with a good many propositions of that kind—if 'proposition' is the right word. We call them clichés because, though Snow clearly feels that he is expressing thought, the thought, considered even for a moment, is seen to be a mere phantom, and Snow's illusion is due to the fact that he is *not* thinking, but resting inertly (though with a sense of power) on vague memories of the way in which he has heard (or seen) such phrases used. They carry for him—he belonging to what he calls a 'culture'—a charge of currency-value which is independent of first-hand, that is, actual, thinking. He would be surprised if he were told they are clichés.

He would be still more surprised to be told it is cliché when, describing the distinctive traits of his scientists, he says: 'they have the future in their bones.' He clearly feels that it has an idiosyncratic speech-raciness that gives his wisdom a genial authority. But it is basic cliché —for Snow's pretensions, more damagingly cliché than the kind of thing I instanced first, for it dismisses the issue, tacitly eliminates the problem, discussion of which would have been the *raison d'être* of the lecture if Snow had been capable of the preoccupation, and the accordant exercise of thought, he advertises.

Such a phrase as 'they have the future in their bones' (and Snow repeats it) cannot be explained as a meaningful proposition, and in that sense has no meaning. It emerges spontaneously from the cultural world to which Snow belongs and it registers uncritically (hence the self-evident force it has for him) its assumptions and attitudes and ignorances. That world, I was on the point of saying, is the world of his 'scientific culture,' but I might equally have said that it is the world of the *New Statesman,* the *Guardian* and the Sunday papers. And Snow rides on an advancing swell of cliché: this exhilarating motion is what he takes for inspired and authoritative thought.

He brings out the intended commendatory force, and the actual large significance, of 'they have the future in their bones' (there is nothing else by way of clarification) by telling us antithetically of the representatives of 'the traditional culture': 'they are natural Luddites.' It is a *general* charge, and he makes quite plain that he includes in it the creators of English literature in the nineteenth century and the twentieth. The upshot is that if you insist on the need for any other kind of concern, entailing forethought, action and provision, about the human future—any other kind of misgiving—than that which talks in terms of productivity, material standards of living, hygienic and technological progress, then you are a Luddite. Snow's position, for all the mess of clichés and sentimental banalities that constitutes his style, is unequivocal.

It might seem an odd position for one who proudly thinks of himself as a major novelist. But I now come to the point when I have again to say, with a more sharply focused intention this time, that Snow not only hasn't in him the beginnings of a novelist; he is utterly without a glimmer of what creative literature is, or why it matters. That significant truth comes home to us, amusingly but finally, when, near his opening, he makes a point of impressing on us that, as himself a creative writer, he is humanly (shall I say?) supremely well qualified—that he emphatically *has* a soul. 'The individual condition of each of us,' he tells us, 'is tragic,' and, by way of explaining that statement, he adds, 'we die alone.' Once he

says 'we live alone,' but in general—for he makes his
point redundantly—he prefers to stress dying; it's more
solemn. He is enforcing a superiority to be recognised in
the scientists: they, he says, 'see no reason why, just because the individual condition is tragic, so must the
social condition be.' For himself, with tragic stoicism,
he says, 'we die alone: all right,' but—which is his message, the sum of his wisdom—'there is social hope.'

He is repetitious, but he develops no explanation further than this. It doesn't occur to him that there is any
need, stultifying as anyone capable of thought can see
the antithesis to be. What *is* the 'social condition' that
has nothing to do with the 'individual condition'? What
is the 'social hope' that transcends, cancels or makes indifferent the inescapable tragic condition of each individual? Where, if not in individuals, is what is hoped for—
a *non*-tragic condition, one supposes—to be located? Or
are we to find the reality of life in hoping for other
people a kind of felicity about which as proposed for
ourselves ('jam,' Snow calls it later—we die alone, but
there's jam to be had first) we have no illusions? Snow's
pompous phrases give us the central and supreme instance of what I have called 'basic cliché.' He takes over
inertly—takes over as a self-evident simple clarity—the
characteristic and disastrous confusion of the civilisation
he is offering to instruct.

It is a confusion to which all creative writers are tacit
enemies. The greatest English writer of our century dealt
with it explicitly—dealt with it again and again, in many
ways, and left to our hand what should be the classical
exposure. But Snow, exhibiting his inwardness with
modern literature by enumerating the writers who above
all matter, leaves Lawrence out (though he offers us
Wyndham Lewis—the brutal and boring Wyndham

Lewis). Lawrence, intent with all his being on the nature
and movement of the civilisation of the West, turned
the intelligence of genius on what I have called the
characteristic confusion. He diagnoses it in his supreme
novel, *Women in Love,* both discursively and by the
poetic means of a great novelist. Concerned with enforcing in relation to what may be called a quintessential
presentment of the modern world the Laurentian maxim
that 'nothing matters but life,' he insists on the truth that
only in living individuals is life there, and individual lives
cannot be aggregated or equated or dealt with quanti-
tatively in any way.

The provocation for the insistence in the place I have
in mind is given by the word 'equality,' and the context
in which the word is introduced may be suggested by
saying that the liberal-idealist sage and social philos-
opher, Sir Joshua Mattheson, who figures in *Women in
Love,* reminds us irresistibly of Bertrand Russell (something of a paradigmatic hero for Snow, who is himself
the spiritual son of H. G. Wells). The Lawrence-like
Birkin of Lawrence's novel says: 'I want every man to
have his share in the world's goods, so that I am rid of
his importunity . . .' The un-Laurentian tone given by
'rid' and 'importunity' belongs to the dramatic Birkin
and the dramatic context, but in what Birkin has just
said we have pure Lawrence: ' "We are all different and
unequal in spirit—it is only the social differences that
are based on accidental material conditions. We are all
abstractly and mathematically equal, if you like. Every
man has hunger and thirst, two eyes, one nose and two
legs. We're all the same in point of number. But spirit-
ually, there is pure difference and neither equality nor
inequality counts." '

The point is intimately related to that which Lawrence

makes when he says that few people live on the spot
where they are—which is equivalent to saying that few
people really live. Snow, in exhorting us to put aside our
individual living and live instead on 'social hope,'
preaches as the way of salvation the characteristic modern mode of refusing to live on the spot where one is.
'Live,' of course, is a word of many possible values, as
great novelists and poets make us know. Snow, refrain-
ing from permitting himself a morbid consciousness of
his individual tragedy, enjoys a personal life, I suspect,
that gives him considerable satisfaction—being a sage, a
familiar of the Corridors of Power, a member of the
Athenæum, a great figure in the Sunday papers, a great
novelist, a maker of young novelists, a maker (perhaps)
of academic careers. He can hardly, for the myriads for
whom he generously entertains 'social hope,' plan or
foresee lives that will be filled with satisfaction and significance in that way. But what primarily calls for emphasis is the poverty of Snow's own ostensible range of
satisfactions—which is a poverty of his own canons, and
of his sense of significance; a poverty in considering
which one finds oneself considering the inadequacy of
his sense of human nature and human need.

The significance of his blankness in the face of literature is immense. It is a significance the more damning
(in relation to his pretensions) because of the conviction
with which he offers himself as an authority on the literature of the present and the past. I didn't exaggerate
when I said that he doesn't know what literature is.
Every pronouncement he makes about it—and he makes
a great many—enforces that truth. Illustrating his notion
of the important kind of relation between art and life,
the writer and the contemporary world, he tells us that
the Russians (he knows all about Russian literature)

'are as ready to cope in art with the processes of produc-
tion as Balzac was with the processes of craft manufacture.' But, for those preoccupied with the problems
Snow confronts us with, unintentionally, literature has
its immediate and crucial relevance because of the kind
of writer who asks, who lives in his art and makes *us*
live, kinds of question that, except as conventional pro-
fundities to which one should sometimes lift one's hat,
seem never to have come within Snow's cognisance (an
effect only emphasised by his 'tragic' and 'we die alone'
—which belong, of course, to the most abject journalism). What for—what ultimately for? What, ultimately,
do men live by? These questions are in and of the creative drive that produces great art in Conrad and Lawrence (to instance two very different novelists of the
century who haven't, one gathers, impressed Snow).

Take, as a simple illustration, Conrad's *The Shadow
Line,* and note—well, note everything, but note particularly the evocation of the young master's inner response
when he first sets eyes on his ship, his first command.
The urgent creative exploring represented by the questions is immeasurably more complex in *Women in Love,*
a comprehensive and intensely 'engaged' study of
modern civilisation. Of course, to such questions there
can't be, in any ordinary sense of the word, 'answers,'
and the effect as of total 'answer' differs as between Conrad and Lawrence, or as between any two great writers.
But life in the civilisation of an age for which such
creative questioning is not done and is not influential on
general sensibility tends characteristically to lack a dimension: it tends to have no depth—no depth against
which it doesn't tacitly protect itself by the habit of unawareness (so Snow enjoins us to do our living in the
dimension of 'social hope'). In coming to terms with

great literature we discover what at bottom we really believe. What for—what ultimately for? what do men live
by—the questions work and tell at what I can only call
a religious depth of thought and feeling. Perhaps, with
my eye on the adjective, I may just recall for you Tom
Brangwen, in *The Rainbow,* watching by the fold in
lambing-time under the night-sky: 'He knew he did not
belong to himself.'

It is characteristic of Snow that 'believe' for him
should be a very simple word. 'Statistically,' he says, 'I
suppose slightly more scientists are in religious terms unbelievers, compared with the rest of the intellectual
world.' There are believers and unbelievers; we all know
what 'religious terms' are; and everything relevant in
relation to the adjective has been said. Snow goes on at
once: 'Statistically, I suppose slightly more scientists are
on the Left in open politics.' The *naïveté* is complete; it
is a *naïveté* indistinguishable from the portentous ignorance. The ignorance is that which appears as historical
ignorance in his account of the Industrial Revolution,
and its consequences, in the nineteenth century. It mani-
fests itself as a terrifying confidence of simplification—
terrifying because of the distortions and falsifications it
entails, and the part it plays in that spirit of practical
wisdom about the human future of which Snow's Rede
Lecture might be called a classic. Disposing with noble
scorn of a wholly imaginary kind of opposition to his
crass Wellsianism, he says (and *this* is his history—and
his logic): 'For, with singular unanimity, in any country
where they have had the chance, the poor have walked
off the land into the factories as fast as the factories
could take them.' This, of course, is mere brute asser-
tion, callous in its irresponsibility. But it is essential to
Snow's wisdom. If one points out that the actual history

has been, with significance for one's apprehension of the full human problem, incomparably and poignantly more complex than that, Snow dismisses one as a 'natural Luddite.' He dismisses so—sees no further significance in—Dickens and Ruskin, and all the writers leading down to Lawrence. Yet—to confine myself to the non-creative writer, about whom the challenged comment is most easily made—it was Ruskin who put into currency the distinction between wealth and well-being, which runs down through Morris and the British Socialist movement to the Welfare State.

But for Ruskin 'well-being' or 'welfare' could not conceivably be matters of merely material standard of living, with the advantages of technology and scientific hygiene. And there we have the gap—the gap that is the emptiness beneath Snow's ignorance—between Snow and not only Ruskin, but the great creative writers of the century before Snow: they don't exist for him; nor does civilisation. Pressing on this ancient university his sense of the urgency of the effort to which we must give ourselves, he says: 'Yet'—in spite, that is, of the 'horror' which, he says, is 'hard to look at straight'—'yet they've proved that common men can show astonishing fortitude in chasing jam tomorrow. Jam today, and men aren't at their most exciting: jam tomorrow, and one often sees them at their noblest. The transformations have also proved something which only the scientific culture can take in its stride. Yet, when we don't take it in our stride, it makes us look silly.'

The callously ugly insensitiveness of the mode of expression is wholly significant. It gives us Snow, who is wholly representative of the world, or culture, to which it belongs. It is the world in which Mr. Macmillan said —or might, taking a tip from Snow, have varied his

phrase by saying—'You never had so much jam'; and
in which, if you are enlightened, you see that the sum of
wisdom lies in expediting the processes which will en-
sure the Congolese, the Indonesians, and Bushmen (no,
not the Bushmen—there aren't enough of them), the
Chinese, the Indians, *their* increasing supplies of jam. It
is the world in which the vital inspiration, the creative
drive, is 'Jam tomorrow' (if you haven't any today) or
(if you have it today) *'More* jam tomorrow.' It is the
world in which, even at the level of the intellectual weeklies, 'standard of living' is an ultimate criterion, its raising an ultimate aim, a matter of wages and salaries and
what you can buy with them, reduced hours of work,
and the technological resources that make your increasing leisure worth having, so that productivity—the
supremely important thing—must be kept on the rise,
at whatever cost to protesting conservative habit.

Don't mistake me. I am not preaching that we should
defy, or try to reverse, the accelerating movement of
external civilisation (the phrase sufficiently explains
itself, I hope) that is determined by advancing technology. Nor am I suggesting that Snow, in so far as he
is advocating improvements in scientific education, is
wrong (I suspect he isn't very original). What I *am* saying is that such a concern is not enough—disastrously
not enough. Snow himself is proof of that, product as he
is of the initial cultural consequences of the kind of
rapid change he wants to see accelerated to the utmost
and assimilating all the world, bringing (he is con-
vinced), provided we are foresighted enough to perceive
that no one now will long consent to be without abundant jam, salvation and lasting felicity to all mankind.

It must be recognised, though, that he doesn't *say*
'salvation' or 'felicity,' but 'jam.' And if 'jam' means

(as it does) the prosperity and leisure enjoyed by our well-to-do working class, then the significant fact not noticed by Snow is that the felicity it represents cannot be regarded by a fully human mind as a matter for happy contemplation. Nor is it felt by the beneficiaries to be satisfying. I haven't time to enlarge on this last point. I will only remark that the observation is not confined to 'natural Luddites': I recently read in the *Economist* a disturbed review of a book by a French sociologist of which the theme is (not a new idea to us) the incapacity of the industrial worker, who—inevitably—looks on real living as reserved for his leisure, to use his leisure in any but essentially passive ways. And this, for me, evokes that total vision which makes Snow's 'social hope' unintoxicating to many of us—the vision of our imminent tomorrow in today's America: the energy, the triumphant technology, the productivity, the high standard of living and the life-impoverishment—the human emptiness; emptiness and boredom craving alcohol—of one kind or another. Who will assert that the average member of a modern society is more fully human, or more alive, than a Bushman, an Indian peasant, or a member of one of those poignantly surviving primitive peoples, with their marvellous art and skills and vital intelligence?

But I will come to the explicit positive note that has all along been my goal (for I am not a Luddite) in this way: the advance of science and technology means a human future of change so rapid and of such kinds, of tests and challenges so unprecedented, of decisions and possible non-decisions so momentous and insidious in their consequences, that mankind—this is surely clear—will need to be in full intelligent possession of its full humanity (and 'possession' here means, not confident ownership of that which belongs to *us*—our property, but a basic living deference towards that to which, opening as it does into the unknown and itself unmeasurable, we know we belong). I haven't chosen to say that mankind will need all its traditional wisdom; that might suggest a kind of conservatism that, so far as I am concerned, is the enemy. What we need, and shall continue to need not less, is something with the livingness of the deepest vital instinct; as intelligence, a power —rooted, strong in experience, and supremely human— of creative response to the new challenges of time; something that is alien to either of Snow's cultures.

His blankness comes out when, intimating (he supposes) that his concern for university reform envisages the total educational function, he tells us how shocking it is that educated people should not be able to appreciate the Shakespeare of science. It simply hasn't occurred to him that to call the master scientific mind (say Rutherford) a Shakespeare is nothing but a cheap journalistic infelicity. He enforces his intention by telling us, after reporting the failure of his literary friends to describe the second law of thermodynamics: 'yet I was asking something which is about the equivalent of *Have you read a work of Shakespeare's?*' There *is* no scientific equivalent of that question; equations between orders so disparate are meaningless—which is not to say that the Neo-Wellsian assurance that proposes them hasn't *its* significance. More largely, Snow exclaims: 'As though the scientific edifice of the physical world were not, in its intellectual depth, complexity and articulation, the most beautiful and wonderful collective work of the mind of man.'

It is pleasant to think of Snow contemplating, daily perhaps, the intellectual depth, complexity and articulation in all their beauty. But there is a prior human achievement of collaborative creation, a more basic work of the mind of man (and more than the mind), one without which the triumphant erection of the scientific edifice would not have been possible: that is, the creation of the human world, including language. It is one we cannot rest on as on something done in the past. It lives in the living creative response to change in the present. I mentioned language because it is in terms of literature that I can most easily make my meaning plain, and because of the answer that seems to me called for by Snow's designs on the university. It is in the study of literature, the literature of one's own language in the first place, that one comes to recognise the nature and priority of the third realm (as, unphilosophically, no doubt, I call it, talking with my pupils), the realm of that which is neither merely private and personal nor public in the sense that it can be brought into the laboratory or pointed to. You cannot point to the poem; it is 'there' only in the re-creative response of individual minds to the black marks on the page. But—a necessary faith—it is something in which minds can meet. The process in which this faith is justified is given fairly enough in an account of the nature of criticism. A judgment is personal or it is nothing; you cannot take over someone else's. The implicit form of a judgment is: This is so, isn't it? The question is an appeal for confirmation that the thing *is* so; implicitly that, though expecting, characteristically, an answer in the form, 'yes, but——,' the 'but' standing for qualifications, reserves, corrections. Here we have a diagram of the collaborative-creative process in which the poem comes to be established as something 'out there,' of common access in what is in some sense a public world. It gives us, too, the nature of the existence of English literature, a living whole that can have its life only in the living present, in the creative response of individuals, who collaboratively renew and perpetuate what they participate in—a cultural community or consciousness. More, it gives us the nature in general of what I have called the 'third realm' to which all that makes us human belongs.

Perhaps I need say no more by way of enforcing my conviction that, for the sake of our humanity—our humanness, for the sake of a human future, we must do, with intelligent resolution and with faith, all we can to maintain the full life in the present—and life is growth —of our transmitted culture. Like Snow I look to the university. Unlike Snow, I am concerned to make it really a university, something (that is) more than a collocation of specialist departments—to make it a centre of human consciousness: perception, knowledge, judgment and responsibility. And perhaps I have sufficiently indicated on what lines I would justify my seeing the centre of a university in a vital English School. I mustn't say more now about what I mean by that, I will only say that the academic is the enemy and that the academic *can* be beaten, as we who ran *Scrutiny* for twenty years proved. We were, and knew we were, Cambridge—the essential Cambridge in spite of Cambridge: that gives you the spirit of what I have in mind. Snow gets on with what he calls 'the traditional culture' better than I do. To impress us with his anti-academic astringency, he tells us of the old Master of Jesus who said about trains running into Cambridge on Sunday: 'It is equally displeasing to God and to myself.' More to the point is that *that,* I remember, was very much the attitude of the academic powers when, thirty years ago,

I wrote a pioneering book on modern poetry that made Eliot a key figure and proposed a new chart, and again when I backed Lawrence as a great writer.

It is assumed, I believe, that work in the scientific departments must be in close touch with the experimental-creative front. In the same way, for the university English School there is a creative front with which, of its function and nature, the School must be in the closest relation. I am not thinking of the fashionable idea that the right qualification for a teaching post is to be a poet—or a commercially successful novelist. I am thinking again of what *Scrutiny* stood—and stands—for: of the creative work it did on the contemporary intellectual-cultural frontier in maintaining the critical function. I must not try now to say more about the way in which such a school would generate in the university a centre of consciousness (and conscience) for our civilisation. I will merely insist that it is not inconceivable that Cambridge might become a place where the culture of the Sunday papers was not taken to represent the best that is thought and known in our time.

If so, it is conceivable, perhaps, that the journalistic addiction of our academic intellectuals—and journalism (in one form or another) is now the menacing disease of university 'English'—might, at Cambridge, be pretty generally recognised for the thing it is. In such a Cambridge the attention I have paid to a Snow would be unnecessary.

SIR CHARLES SNOW'S REDE LECTURE

by Michael Yudkin

S IR CHARLES SNOW'S account of a cultural dichotomy
is more tendentious than explicit; his main concern
is to express the problem that he sees and to expose
its peripheral consequences, rather than to explain its
causes in detail. What central argument there is proceeds mainly by anecdote—High Table conversations
and inconsequential stories of famous men figure promi-
nently—and the explicit pronouncement is rare:

> I believe the intellectual life of the whole of western
> society is increasingly being split into two polar groups
> . . . at one pole we have the literary intellectuals . . .
> at the other scientists.

From this and a few other passages, however, we gather
that Sir Charles believes the present cultural polariza-
tion to be disastrous, both intellectually and practically,
and that someone, somehow, should do something about
it.

One would have hoped that Snow, having hit on 'The
Two Cultures' as a title for his lecture, would have gone
on to make it clear what he understands by a culture.
Obviously he does not mean to imply that the body of

men whom he classes together in a cultural group auto-
matically share an interest and comprehension of one
another's work; nor presumably are we intended to take
the word 'culture' as denoting a complex of shared assumptions. Sir Charles himself makes a half-apology for
his lack of precision, but curiously enough he is more
concerned with the number two than the term 'culture.'

> I have been argued with by non-scientists of strong
> down-to-earth interests. Their view is that it is an over-
> simplification, and that if one is going to talk in these
> terms there ought to be at least three cultures . . .
> J. H. Plumb, Alan Bullock and some of my American
> sociological friends have said that they vigorously re-
> fuse to be corralled in a cultural box with people they
> wouldn't be seen dead with.

In dismissing these protests, Sir Charles is also loosening the meaning of the term 'traditional culture,' which
he constantly opposes to 'scientific culture.' The nature
of the 'traditional culture' thus becomes rather mysteri-
ous: it starts as the preserve of literary intellectuals, but
soon becomes the whole range of non-scientific intellectual activity. Inevitably this vagueness leads to a confusion disappointing in a writer apparently so urgently
concerned with the problem.

The disclaimer of J. H. Plumb, Alan Bullock and Sir
Charles's American sociological friends is not the only
objection that can be made against the concept of the
two cultures. By making the division within our culture
such a simple one, Sir Charles implies, though one supposes not intentionally, that communication within each
separated part is on a satisfactorily high level. In other
words, by concentrating attention on the gap between

scientific and non-scientific intellectual effort, he by-
passes the many gaps within each 'culture.' Snow con-
fesses himself astounded to discover that the average
graduate in science cannot read Dickens; but has he
examined how many graduates in, say, law or economics
are in the same condition? It is a failing of some specialists in every field to believe that their subjects
comprise all worthwhile intellectual activity, a misappre-
hension which the faculty structure of the universities
tends to promote. Thus when Sir Charles says

> the whole literature of the traditional culture doesn't
> seem to them (scientists) relevant to (their) interests.
> They are, of course, dead wrong. As a result, their
> imaginative understanding is less than it could be. They
> are self-impoverished.

we might well ask whether we are to believe that only
scientists are impoverished in this way. Do those members of the 'traditional culture' who do not specifically
study literature, or music, or the fine arts enrich themselves by contact with them? Do they not, like the scientists, believe works of art to be irrelevant to their
interests? There are, regrettably, dozens of cultures, in
Sir Charles's use of the term, even if the gap between the
scientist and the non-scientist is probably the widest.

There are three stages to Sir Charles's argument: first,
that there exists a mutual failure of contact and comprehension between scientists and non-scientists. Next,
that this failure is at least unfortunate, and probably
dangerous. Finally, he claims that it is possible to find
ways of crossing this chasm of understanding, and that
all efforts should be made to close the gap. The first of

these propositions cannot be seriously doubted; for scientists and non-scientists to understand one another's work requires a huge stretching of the intellect, and the effort needed becomes constantly greater. The idea that this is universally to be regretted has scarcely been disputed; but it is the conclusion of the argument—that it is possible to make a significant improvement in the intellectual relationship—that is open to the most serious criticism.

Sir Charles makes some play with examples of mutual incomprehension. In his experience, many scientists find Dickens unintelligible, while almost all those who have been educated in the traditional culture are unable to define mass or acceleration. This sort of comparison is frequently made; it is of doubtful use and often misleads, for implied in it is an equivalence between an artistic experience and a scientific finding. To read Dickens, or to hear Mozart, or to see a Titian can be in itself a rewarding activity; but to find out what is meant by acceleration is to gain a piece of factual information which in itself has no value. It is unfortunate that Sir Charles should stress, as desirable for the non-scientist, the acquisition of scientific knowledge. What would be of value is an understanding of the process and manner of scientific thinking; for it is the nature of scientific judgment, the habit of a peculiar form of critical thought, which is characteristic of the scientific culture, which makes scientific work a worthwhile intellectual activity and, incidentally, which would give science some value as a disciplined study for the non-scientist.

If the chasm between artist and scientist can be bridged, then, Sir Charles implies, a possible method of constructing this bridge would be a decrease in specialization of school studies—a specialization which he ascribes (on the basis of conversations with schoolmasters) to the Oxford and Cambridge scholarship examinations. One may wonder how far these examinations are responsible for the over-specialization, and how far it is the result of considerations of convenience in designing the school syllabus. However, it is certainly possible to reduce the intensity of specialization for scientists. Why should those studying science not read Dickens, and Shakespeare, and Homer, and Virgil? Why should they not be taught the history of music and painting and architecture? For it is in the nature of at any rate some of the art available in Europe that it needs no specialized training for its appreciation. The scientists could certainly bridge Sir Charles's gulf.

But it can only be a one-way bridge. For the non-scientist, an understanding of science rests not on the acquisition of scientific knowledge, but on scientific habits of thought and method. No matter how many scientific subjects a child studies to 'O' level, no matter how many lectures on scientific method he attends, or how much he reads of Bacon or Descartes or Hume or Mill, he will never understand the nature of scientific procedure until he reads at least a Natural Science course for undergraduates. Even this intensive study of a science would be far less valuable than a piece of scientific research—for it is in the inferences from experimental data, the building of hypotheses and the planning of experiments, that a full scientific education lies.

Sir Charles, on the other hand, pursues the falsely optimistic idea of an age of Leonardos. Though he is apparently outstanding in his generation in feeling equally at home within both the 'cultures,' literary and scientific, he is capable of strange prejudices. One may well be dismayed at the level of sensibility and understanding displayed by this sort of passage:

> I remember being cross-examined by a scientist of distinction. 'Why do most writers take on social opinions which would have been thought distinctly uncivilised and démodé at the time of the Plantagenets? Wasn't that true of most of the famous twentieth-century writers? Yeats, Pound, Wyndham Lewis, nine out of ten of those who have dominated literary sensibility in our time—weren't they not only politically silly, but politically wicked? Didn't the influence of all they represent bring Auschwitz that much nearer?'
>
> I thought at the time, and I still think, that the correct answer was not to defend the indefensible. It was no use saying that Yeats, according to friends whose judgment I trust, was a man of singular magnanimity of character, as well as a great poet. It was no use denying the facts, which are broadly true. The honest answer was that there is, in fact, a connection, which literary persons were culpably slow to see, between some kinds of early twentieth-century art and the most imbecile expressions of anti-social feeling. That was one reason, among many, why some of us turned our backs on the art and tried to hack out a new or different way for ourselves.

But if Snow, the writer, can so easily dismiss Yeats, Pound and Lewis, Snow, the scientist, exhibits a limitation no less remarkable. For him, science includes only the physical sciences. Rutherford and Eddington, Jeans and J. J. Thomson are at home in his pages. Bragg meets the author on a railway station; Cockcroft's visit to Russia supplies the material for an anecdote. But where are the biologists, the biochemists and the physiologists? Adrian receives the courtesy of a mention, but where are Haldane and Barcroft? Where is Hopkins, surely as distinguished and as colourful a figure in his field as was Rutherford in his?

These remarks are not intended as debating points. Sir Charles is, after all, conspicuous in his attempt to unite the 'two cultures.' Nor could he fairly be charged with even average narrow-mindedness: his novels, for instance, are dusted with references to Proust—a writer very different from Snow in method, style and milieu. But if a man of Sir Charles's range of interests can nonetheless reveal such serious limitations, is there any reason to be optimistic about the broadness of mind of the average scientist or artist? When the totality of knowledge is so immense that even scientists working in the same field can unwittingly repeat each other's published work, how much hope can Sir Charles maintain of a correspondence across the gap between scientists and non-scientists? The most that might be expected would be that the education of children—whether they subsequently become scientists or not—should include an awareness of the most valuable achievements in our literary and artistic culture. For the reasons that I have outlined, the converse—a useful scientific education of non-scientists—is not a practical aim.

But the fact that the arts student cannot be educated into the scientific method is not as disastrous as Sir Charles imagines. There are, after all, only two possible aims for education; one is entirely practical, a matter of teaching what is necessary for living in a community, while the other is less tangible, a matter of helping the student to become a more sociable, or aware, or sympathetic, person. Now having strayed into the use of terms as imprecise as those I have criticised in Sir Charles Snow, I must add a gloss. Even though there may be no general agreement about the meaning of sympathy or artistic awareness, there would be substantial agreement about the existence of qualities in the personality which it is good to encourage and develop. One such quality is (in the most general terms) the ability to form satisfactory relationships with other people; another is an awareness and feeling for the arts; a third is the training of the intellectual faculty, through the rigour of such studies as grammar or logic. What is not to be included in a list of these qualities, and what, consequently, is not an educational function, is an increase of mere knowledge without regard to its purpose.

It is thus possible to make out a substantial list of reasons why the study of literature, of history, or of art, is to be desired in a general curriculum. It is possible, too, to understand the necessity of teaching elementary science to those who are to be scientists—and, since it is not known at an early age which children will make a career in science, it is desirable to include elementary science among the subjects taught to all children. But it is idle to deplore the lack of scientific knowledge in specialists in other fields. To understand what is meant by mass or acceleration can certainly be of no practical help to a student of classical literature, nor could it have the more subtle effect on the personality that might be its other justification. It would be, strictly, useless knowledge.*

* This argument has one important consequence which lies outside the academic context within which Sir Charles's discussion is centred. It is necessary for politicians to be sufficiently trained in science to understand the nature and meaning of the scientific advice which they receive. It is probable, for instance, that Government ministers never properly understood the controversial question of the hazards of nuclear tests. Such understanding would demand not a technical acquaintance with an individual scientific problem, but the ability to evaluate scien-

If one were to ask Sir Charles Snow why he thought scientists should read Shakespeare he would reply something like this: 'Apart from any consideration of beauty of form or language, Shakespeare's analysis and exploration of characters and their interaction shows such unusual awareness and insight that a study of his work is capable of enriching the personality and the vicarious experience of his readers.' If one asked him why he believed that non-scientists should know something of modern physics, his answer would be less predictable, but would probably be based on a feeling that every educated person should be aware of the extent of intellectual activity covered by science. Sir Charles drops a tiny clue to his probable response in the following passage.

> It is bizarre how very little of twentieth-century science has been assimilated into twentieth-century art. Now and then one used to find poets conscientiously using scientific expressions, and getting them wrong— there was a time when 'refraction' kept cropping up in verse in a mystifying fashion, and when 'polarised light' was used as though writers were under the illusion that it was a specially admirable kind of light.
>
> Of course that isn't the way that science could be any good to art. It has got to be assimilated along with, and as part and parcel of, the whole of our mental experience, and used as naturally as the rest.

This is one of those puzzling statements that one would dearly love to see expanded. Just how does Sir

---

tific evidence, especially when the evidence is scanty; this reasoning implies that ministers responsible for scientific decisions should be themselves trained scientists. At present, politicians tend to rely on the opinions of those advisers who state their views with far more dogmatism than the evidence warrants.

Charles believe that the assimilation of science as part of the mental experience of the artist can improve his work? Writers, for instance, are accustomed to examine personal relationships in their work; they draw on their experience of people and their understanding of the interaction of minds and characters. Could the concept of the expanding universe aid the novelist or the playwright by enhancing his sympathetic awareness of human beings? Or does Sir Charles believe that a poet examining the effect of the threat of modern warfare on the behaviour of his contemporaries will create a finer poem if he is aware of the mechanism of the hydrogen bomb?

A similar attitude is apparent in Snow's complaint of the lack of communication between the 'two cultures.' The complaint itself is not an unusual one, but it is odd to find such a limited idea of communication in a successful novelist. Sir Charles insists that a student of literature should acquaint himself with science, and that a scientist should read Dickens; but one would like to ask how Sir Charles envisages such exchange of knowledge as an aid to communication. Is communication the intelligibility of one don's conversation at High Table to another? Was this the notion of communication held by Tolstoy or D. H. Lawrence? Surely it is a subtler and more sensitive affair, a deep and genuinely personal understanding. Snow believes that 'at the heart of thought and creation we are letting some of our best chances go by default.' It is, for him, the lack of communication between the 'two cultures' that is responsible for these wasted chances. But when we seek an example of this lack, we are told of an experiment at Columbia by Yang and Lee.

If there were any serious communication between the two cultures, this experiment would have been talked about at every High Table in Cambridge.

It would seem unfair to accuse Sir Charles of a depersonalised, scientific view of communication on the basis of his lecture alone. But an astonishingly similar outlook is evident from his novels—and the novel is surely the form in which communication, the relationship of people and their emotions, must be most sensitively examined. Snow's most recent novel, *The Affair,* exemplifies his method. The whole book is an account of a situation, in which the characters are portrayed not as individuals but as types, as if masked for a mime. Each character receives on appearance a paragraph or two of description or biography, so that it is possible to predict the rôle each will play in the action; none develops beyond the limits set out at the beginning. Through this whole highly stylized story the author-narrator exhibits a clinical, academic interest in the moving of the drama. Throughout the book there is no examination of *personal* communication.

If for Sir Charles communication is an abstract, impersonal affair, education is an abstract, quantitative and similarly impersonal matter. He does not seem to make the distinction between knowledge and enhancement of the personality. He seems never to ask himself 'knowledge for what?' For him an educated man is a man who knows a great deal, and a better educated man is a man who knows more. The acquisition of knowledge is, it seems, its own end; or, as he says in another context, 'A fact is a fact is a fact.' The following passage, an important one in the lecture, indicates his preoccupation:

A good many times I have been present at gatherings of people who, by the standards of the traditional culture, are thought highly educated and who have with considerable gusto been expressing their incredulity at the illiteracy of scientists. Once or twice I have been provoked and have asked the company how many of them could describe the Second Law of Thermodynamics. The response was cold: it was also negative. Yet I was asking something which is about the scientific equivalent of: Have you read a work of Shakespeare's?

This idea is central to Sir Charles's argument; it equates scientific knowledge and artistic experience. The values behind such an equation are, in themselves, curious; but their consequences are still more grave. For further study of Sir Charles's lecture makes it clear that the problem of the two cultures is not really foremost in his mind. Having touched his cap to the serious question implied in the title of his lecture, he becomes most deeply concerned with another subject; and this is a problem which, if solved by the methods that Sir Charles suggests, must make the gap between the 'two cultures' even less easy to bridge than it is at present.

It is barely possible to read a newspaper without seeing an appeal by a politician, or an industrialist, or a university teacher, for more scientists, larger sums of money for technical research, or an expansion of the universities. It is this clamour which Sir Charles, in the last part of his lecture, is concerned to increase. In fairness, his motives must be distinguished from the more usual pressures of materialism to which we have grown accustomed. Sir Charles does not frighten us with claims that Britain is lagging in the space race; he does not urge us to worry that our prestige may suffer through failure to manufacture nuclear weapons; he does not even press students of the 'traditional culture' to divert to science and thus help to defend our civilised values against the march of communism. His motives are more generous: he asks us to provide the huge investment, in men and capital, that is necessary to industrialise the under-developed countries outside Europe and to save their populations from starvation.

It would be cynical to dismiss so compelling and altruistic a suggestion with a quibble; one cannot sneer at a man who sincerely and boldly raises a uniquely important problem in this way:

> Most of our fellow human beings are underfed and die before their time. In the crudest terms, *that* is the social condition.

But what one longs to ask Sir Charles is his purpose in raising it in the context of a discussion of the 'two cultures,' for it invites the comment that Sir Charles must realise his two aims to be incompatible. He must know that a scientist is as technically competent, as able to 'pass on what he knows and do an honest technical job,' whether he is acquainted with Dickens or not. He must also be aware that, if it is possible to train a technician adequately in two years, to educate him more broadly outside his field for five years is a luxury which no government distressed by a shortage of technicians will contemplate. Moreover, Sir Charles must be acquainted with the far from altruistic reasons that have urged our masters to call for the scientific and technical manpower which will make our country powerful and respected. The danger is that his appeal will seem to add to that almost irresistible weight of demands, and to condone that outlook which sees children as so much material to be bent to the fulfilling of policy, rather than as people whom education is intended to benefit.

It would have been instructive to hear from Sir Charles how this large requirement of scientists could be met. Can there be any method which does not involve the direction of able children away from the study of the 'traditional culture' which one half of Snow admires? We see the beginning of this process in the loosening of the requirements for scientists' matriculation at Oxford and Cambridge, and in the foundation of new universities and colleges with an unusually high proportion of science students. If Sir Charles is concerned about the lack of awareness of the 'traditional culture' among scientists, why does he not speak out against such methods of narrowing their intellectual environment? Sir Charles's two aims—more scientists *and* a generally broader education—do not seem to be compatible within any foreseeable development of our educational policy. Instead, his lecture will succeed in giving comfort only to those who wish to increase the number of science graduates and care nothing for the broader requirements of their education.

There is a real danger that the problem of the 'two cultures' may gradually cease to exist. There will be no building of a bridge across the gap, no appearance of modern Leonardos, no migration of scientists to literature. Instead there will be the atrophy of the traditional culture, and its gradual annexation by the scientific— annexation not of territory but of men. It may not be long before only a single culture remains.